YOUNG ENGINEERS

Building Vehicles that Fly

by Tammy Enz

Y0-CAV-035

capstone

Edited by Adrian Vigliano
Designed by Philippa Jenkins
Picture research by Svetlana Zhurkin
Production by Katy LaVigne
Originated by Capstone Global Library Ltd

21 20 19 18 17
10 9 8 7 6 5 4 3

Library of Congress Cataloging-in-Publication Data
Library of Congress Cataloging-in-Publication data is available on the Library of Congress website.

ISBN: 9781484637470 (library binding)
ISBN: 9781484637517 (pbk.)

Acknowledgments
The author and publisher are grateful to the following for permission to reproduce copyright material: Capstone Studio: Karon Dubke, cover, 8, 9, 10, 11, 14, 15, 18, 19, 22, 23, 26, 27; Shutterstock: Andrey Khachatryan, 13, byvalet, 5, iliuta goean, 21, Philip Arno Photography, 25 (bottom), Phillip Rubino, 29, tobkatrina, 7, Vibrant Image Studio, 17

We would like to thank Harold Pratt for his help in the preparation of this book.

Every effort has been made to contact copyright holders of any material reproduced in this book. Any omissions will be rectified in subsequent printings if notice is given to the publisher.

All the Internet addresses (URLs) given in this book were valid at the time of going to press. However, due to the dynamic nature of the Internet, some addresses may have changed, or sites may have changed or ceased to exist since publication. While the author and publisher regret any inconvenience this may cause readers, no responsibility for any such changes can be accepted by either the author or the publisher.

Printed in the United States of America.
082017 010678RP

Table of Contents

Some words are shown in bold, **like this.** You can find out what they mean by looking in the glossary.

Forces in Flight

Soaring the skies is an amazing feat. But whether a huge airplane or a tiny bird, all fliers deal with the four forces of flight. **Weight** and **drag** try to pull fliers from the sky or slow them down. But **thrust** and **lift** fight these forces to keep planes and birds aloft.

lift

thrust

drag

weight

Airplane designers carefully balance four forces to allow planes to soar in the sky.

Weight

It takes extra force to keep heavier objects in the air. So most airplanes are made from the lightest material possible, usually **aluminum**. Aluminum is lightweight but not as strong as some other materials. So sometimes **composite** materials are used. Composite materials are a mixture of two materials. The composite is stronger than either material on its own.

Engineers are always looking for ways to make airplanes lighter.

Experiment with Weight

In this experiment you can see how extra weight takes extra force to keep aloft.

You will need:
- Tape
- Small toy
- A sheet of construction paper
- 4 pieces of string about 3 feet (1 meter) long

1. Tape one end of each string to a corner of the paper.

2. Tape the other ends of the strings to the top of a door frame. Make sure the paper hangs flat.

3. Blow on the paper from beneath. How hard must you blow to get the paper to rise?

4. Place the toy on the paper.

5. Now how hard must you blow to move the paper?

Experiment with Composites

Papier-mâché is a composite you can easily make.

You will need:

- Mixing bowl and spoon
- ½ cup (60 grams) flour
- ½ cup (.12 liter) water
- Paintbrush
- Sheet of plastic
- 20-30 newspaper strips about 1 inch (3 centimeters) wide x 6 inches (15 cm) long

1. Stir the flour and water together in the bowl until smooth.

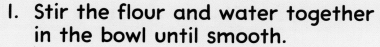

2. Paint a thin layer of plaster on the sheet of plastic.
3. Lay 5 newspaper strips side by side on the plaster. Paint on another layer of plaster.
4. Lay 5 more strips crosswise on top.
5. Repeat with another layer.
6. Paint a thick layer of plaster on another spot on the plastic.
7. Allow to dry overnight.
8. Peel off the papier-mâché and plaster.
9. Now compare a fresh newspaper strip, the dried plaster, and the dried papier-mâché. Test the materials to see which is strongest.

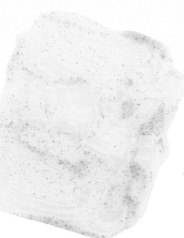

Drag

As fliers try to push through the air, drag slows them down. Drag is air's push against something as it moves. The faster an object moves, the more drag slows it down. You feel drag when you run very fast. A plane's shape can help lessen drag. Round and tapered surfaces help air move past the plane to reduce drag.

Engineers make planes as smooth as possible to lessen drag.

Experiment with Drag

See how an airplane's shape affects drag in this experiment.

You will need:

- 2 sheets of paper
- Ruler
- Scissors
- 2 paper clips

1. Crease one paper in half lengthwise.

2. Open it and fold the top corners into the crease. Fold the corners in again.

3. Fold the paper in half along the crease.

4. Fold each flap down to make wings.

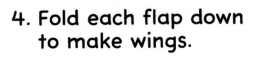

5. Repeat steps 1-4 with the other paper to make another plane.

6. Measure and cut 5 inches (13 cm) off the nose of one plane to make its front blunt.

7. Attach a paper clip to the nose of each plane. Test your planes by flying each. Try to launch the planes identically. Which flies better?

Some fliers count on drag to help them. **Parachutes** help skydivers move slowly through the air. The parachutes spread out to capture air and increase drag. If you jump from a plane without a parachute you fall to the ground at over 125 miles (200 kilometers) per hour. With a parachute you fall at only about 12 miles (19 km) per hour.

With a parachute, drag can save your life!

Make a Parachute

Test out drag by building your own parachute.

You will need:

- A small plastic toy
- 4 18 inch-(46 cm-) long pieces of thread
- An 18 inch (46 cm) square of plastic cut from a garbage bag

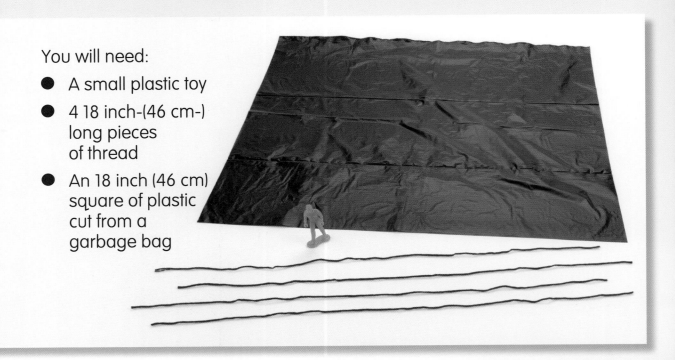

1. Lightly toss the toy into the air. How quickly does it fall?

2. Tie one end of each thread around a corner of the plastic.
3. Tie the other ends of the threads to the toy.
4. Gather the plastic and toy in your hand and toss lightly into the air. Does the parachute help the toy land more slowly?

Thrust

Planes and birds create thrust to fight against weight and drag. Thrust is the force that moves these fliers forward. Birds flap their wings to create thrust. Planes use burning gases to thrust them forward. As gases push out of the back of the plane, the plane moves forward.

Everything that flies must create thrust to stay in the air.

21

Experiment with Thrust

See how moving gas thrusts a balloon forward with this experiment.

You will need:

- 2 pieces of a drinking straw 1 inch (3 cm) long
- A piece of string about 6 feet (2 m) long
- 2 chairs
- Balloon
- Tape

1. Thread the straw pieces onto the string.

2. Tie each end of the string to a chair. Move the chairs apart so the string is stretched tightly.

3. Blow up the balloon.

4. Holding the balloon closed, tape one of the straws to the fattest part of the balloon. Loosely tape the other straw to the neck of the balloon.

5. Starting at one end of the string, let the balloon go. As the gas leaves the balloon, what happens?

Lift

Thrust moves planes forward. But lift keeps planes aloft. An airplane's wings are specially shaped to create lift. Their tapered shape is called an **airfoil**. As a plane thrusts forward, airfoil-shaped wings change the air's direction and lift a plane up. Bird's wings are airfoils too.

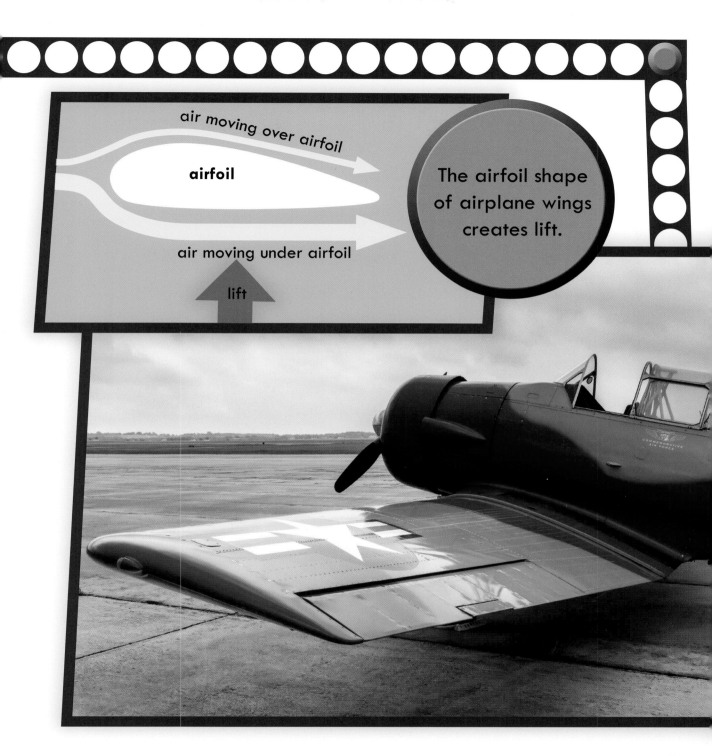

air moving over airfoil

airfoil

air moving under airfoil

lift

The airfoil shape of airplane wings creates lift.

Experiment with Airfoils

Try this experiment to see an airfoil in action.

You will need:

- A 6-inch (15-cm) square piece of construction paper
- Tape

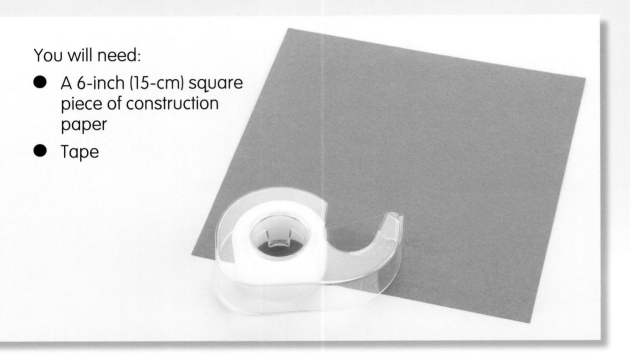

1. Bend the paper so that two edges are touching. Leave the folded edge rounded. Tape the edges together.

2. Place the airfoil on a table. Hold your hands behind it to prevent it from blowing away.

3. Gently blow directly at the taped edge. Does anything happen?

4. Now flip the airfoil. Blow at the rounded edge. Now does the airfoil lift? Try flattening the bottom of your airfoil then blowing on the rounded edge again. Does this change how it moves?

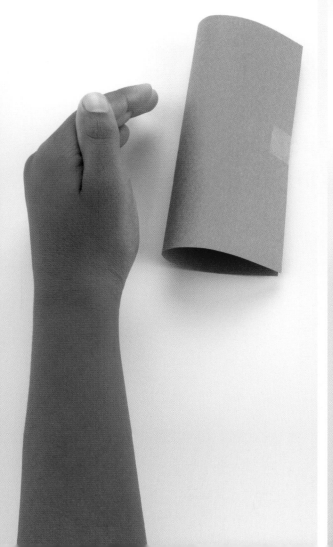

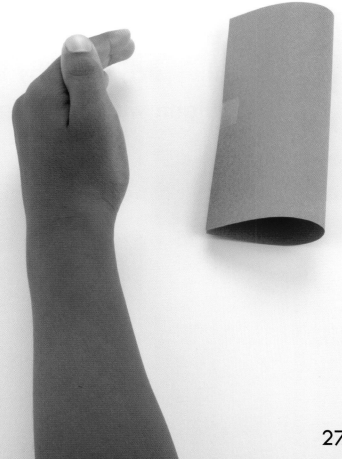

Flight seems baffling. But it is less so when you understand the forces of flight. Think about these forces the next time you see a plane take off or a bird fly by. Know that they stay aloft by balancing the forces of flight: weight, drag, lift, and thrust.

Engineers work hard each day to design the next great airplane.

Glossary

airfoil—a rounded wing that creates lift

aluminum—a light metal

composite—a material made from two different materials

drag—slowing force from air

lift—rising force caused by a moving airfoil

parachute—cloth that fills with air to slow a falling object

thrust—pushing force

weight—the heaviness of something

Find Out More

Books

Brown, Jordan. *How Airplanes Get from Here... to There!*
Science of Fun Stuff. New York: Simon Spotlight,
2016.

Farndon, John. *Stickmen's Guide to Aircraft*. Minneapolis:
Hungry Tomato, 2016.

Riggs, Kate. *Helicopters*. Mankato, Minn.: Creative
Education, 2015.

Internet sites

Facthound offers a safe, fun way to find Internet sites
related to this book. All of the sites on Facthound have
been researched by our staff.

Here's all you do:
Visit *www.facthound.com*
Type in this code: 9781484637470

Index